New York, June 1800

It is 7 o'clock on a warm summer morning. A ship is arriving in New York. Its name is the *Red Rose*. Two of the people on it are Sam Tinker and his daughter Jenny. Sam and Jenny are English, but now they are starting a new life in America. "Look, Dad!" says Jenny. "We're here. We're really *here*!"

The Tinkers say goodbye to all their friends. Then they leave the *Red Rose*. There are lots of people, horses and carts beside the ship. Sam looks at them. "Yes, we're here," he thinks. "But now what? We haven't got any money." He stops a young man with a green coat. "Excuse me," he says. "I'm looking for a job." The man turns to his right. "Talk to Jack Crane," he answers.

Jack Crane is a farmer. He has a long, thin face and only three fingers on his right hand. He listens to Sam's story. Then he takes off his hat. "OK," he says, "you can *both* have jobs. I need a new man to work in the fields. And we want someone to help in the kitchen, too – isn't that right, Blue Sky?" There is an Indian girl on top of the cart. "Yes," she says and smiles at Jenny.

Two hours later the Tinkers leave New York with Jack Crane and Blue Sky. They are both very happy. "How far is it to your farm, Mr Crane?" asks Sam. "Eighty kilometres," Jack Crane answers.

They drive all afternoon. Jenny is sitting next to Sam. She is tired, but she does not want to sleep. "This is America," she thinks, " ... and now I'm American."

After six hours Jack Crane stops the cart.
"Well ... there it is," he says. Jenny stands up.
It is evening now and the sun is going down. In front of them there are lots of beautiful yellow fields and a big farmhouse. Jenny looks to her left. "Where's that smoke coming from?" she asks. "That's the Indian village," answers Blue Sky. "My family lives there."

The next day the Tinkers start work. Jenny helps Blue Sky in the farmhouse. First the two girls cook everyone's breakfast. Then they make all the beds. After that they clean the kitchen floor. At the same time Sam is working in the fields. After four or five hours he stops for a minute. "What are you stopping for?" asks Jack Crane. "Come on – get back to work!"

Sam and Jenny have only one free day every week – Sunday. It's Blue Sky's free day, too. That is when she visits her family. One Sunday Jenny goes with her. She makes a lot of new friends. She meets the village Chief, too – Silver Cloud. He has a beautiful wife and a young son. After that first visit, Jenny often goes to the village. She starts to learn some Indian words, too.

Jenny is always happy with her new Indian friends. But she is not happy on the farm. Sam is unhappy, too. "I don't want to work here on Jack Crane's farm any more," he says one evening. "I want to work on *my* farm, Tinkers Farm." "I know, Dad," Jenny answers. Then she thinks, "But *how*? We can't buy any land. Jack Crane pays us only two dollars a week."

Four days later Jenny and Blue Sky are making the beds. Suddenly they hear something. Two men are shouting. Jenny looks out of the window. She can see Jack Crane and her father in front of the farmhouse. Jack Crane's face is very red. "*Do* it!" he shouts. "No, I'm not going to," Sam shouts back. "It's Sunday and I don't work on Sundays. *You* do it!"

Jenny runs downstairs and out of the house. There is a strong wind and it is raining.

"What's happening?" she asks her father. "We're leaving in the morning," Sam answers. He is walking very fast. Jenny looks at him. "But ... how are we going to *eat*? We haven't got any money." Sam does not answer. His eyes are cold and hard.

That evening Jenny and Blue Sky go to the Indian
village. "This is going to be my last visit." Jenny thinks.
Blue Sky is sad, too. She does not want to lose her friend.
The two girls say nothing for twenty minutes. Then
Blue Sky stops her horse. She can see something in the
river to their right. It is a small boy. "Help!" he is
shouting. "I can't swim. Help me! Please!"

"It's the Chief's son!" says Blue Sky. "What are we going to ... " But before she can say another word, Jenny gets off her horse.
"I'm coming," she shouts. Then she jumps into the cold river. "Help!" shouts the boy. Jenny swims to him. His head is going under the water. She puts one arm around him. "It's OK," she says. "You're safe now."

Half an hour later Jenny and Blue Sky arrive at the Indian village. The Chief comes to meet them. "But ... I don't understand," he says to Blue Sky. "Why is my son with you? And why are he and the English girl wet?!" Blue Sky tells him the story. After that the Chief is very happy. He smiles at Jenny. "How can I thank you?" he says. "Please ... let me give you something. *Anything.*"

At 9 o'clock Sam is putting some boots into a bag.
"What's going to happen tomorrow?" he thinks.
Suddenly the door opens. It is Jenny. "Come with me,
Dad," she says. "I want to show you something." Sam
looks at his daughter. Her eyes are bright and she is
smiling. "What are you talking about?" he asks. "There
isn't time for any questions," says Jenny. "Come on."

She takes her father to a hill. At the top she says,
"Look! Can you see that land over there?" "Yes," Sam
answers. Then Jenny tells him about Silver Cloud's son.
After she finishes, Sam says, "You mean ... ?" "Yes,"
Jenny smiles at her father. "The Indians are giving us
our own farm ... 'TINKERS FARM'. Oh Dad, isn't it
wonderful? Now we can *really* start a new life."

Questions

1. What nationality are the Tinkers? (*page 1*)
2. Who tells Sam to talk to Jack Crane? (*page 2*)
3. How far is Jack Crane's farm from New York? (*page 4*)
4. Where does Blue Sky's family live? (*page 5*)
5. What does Jenny do on her first morning? (*page 6*)
6. Who is Silver Cloud? (*page 7*)
7. How much does Jack Crane pay the Tinkers? (*page 8*)
8. Blue Sky sees someone in the river. Who? (*page 12*)
9. What do the Indians give Jenny and Sam? (*page 15*)

Puzzle

Here are five American cities and five states too. Do you know which city is in which state? Write A, B, C, etc in the boxes.

1 San Francisco ☐   2 Phoenix ☐   3 Boston ☐
4 Denver ☐   5 Chicago ☐

A Colorado   **B** Illinois   **C** California   **D** Massachusetts
E Arizona

Ideas

1. Find out about *modern* American Indians. What are the names of the different groups or "tribes"? Where do they live? What kind of clothes do they wear?
2. Write a short poem about New York today. Use one of the words below at the end of each line:
   small/tall   cars/stars   high/sky   loud/crowd